MAD LIPS®

For the Fans

Taylor Swift Edition

MAD LIBS
An imprint of Penguin Random House LLC, New York

First published in the United States of America by Mad Libs,
an imprint of Penguin Random House LLC, New York, 2024

Mad Libs format and text copyright © 2024 by Penguin Random House LLC

Concept created by Roger Price & Leonard Stern

Cover illustration by Jacqueline Li

Photo credits: cover: (disco ball) Elizaveta Bochkova/iStock/Getty Images,
(glitter) SSpino/iStock/Getty Images, (microphone) Mariia Akimova/iStock/Getty Images;
interior: (heart hands) mhatzapa/iStock/Getty Images

Visit us online at penguinrandomhouse.com.

Printed in the United States of America

ISBN 9780593887912
1 3 5 7 9 10 8 6 4 2
COMR

MAD LIBS

INSTRUCTIONS

MAD LIBS® is a game for people who don't like games!
It can be played by one, two, three, four, or forty.

• RIDICULOUSLY SIMPLE DIRECTIONS

In this tablet you will find stories containing blank spaces where words
are left out. One player, the READER, selects one of these stories. The
READER does not tell anyone what the story is about. Instead, he/she asks
the other players, the WRITERS, to give him/her words. These words are
used to fill in the blank spaces in the story.

• TO PLAY

The READER asks each WRITER in turn to call out a word—an adjective or
a noun or whatever the space calls for—and uses them to fill in the blank
spaces in the story. The result is a MAD LIBS® game.

When the READER then reads the completed MAD LIBS® game to the other
players, they will discover that they have written a story that is fantastic,
screamingly funny, shocking, silly, crazy, or just plain dumb—depending
upon which words each WRITER called out.

• EXAMPLE (Before and After)

"_____!" he said _____
EXCLAMATION   ADVERB

as he jumped into his convertible _____ and
                                        NOUN

drove off with his _____ wife.
                         ADJECTIVE

"_____OUCH_____!" he said _____HAPPILY_____
EXCLAMATION   ADVERB

as he jumped into his convertible _____CAT_____ and
                                        NOUN

drove off with his _____BRAVE_____ wife.
                         ADJECTIVE

In case you have forgotten what adjectives, adverbs, nouns, and verbs are, here is a quick review:

An ADJECTIVE describes something or somebody. *Lumpy, soft, ugly, messy,* and *short* are adjectives.

An ADVERB tells how something is done. It modifies a verb and usually ends in "ly." *Modestly, stupidly, greedily,* and *carefully* are adverbs.

A NOUN is the name of a person, place, or thing. *Sidewalk, umbrella, bridle, bathtub,* and *nose* are nouns.

A VERB is an action word. *Run, pitch, jump,* and *swim* are verbs. Put the verbs in past tense if the directions say PAST TENSE. *Ran, pitched, jumped,* and *swam* are verbs in the past tense.

When we ask for A PLACE, we mean any sort of place: a country or city (*Spain, Cleveland*) or a room (*bathroom, kitchen*).

An EXCLAMATION or SILLY WORD is any sort of funny sound, gasp, grunt, or outcry, like *Wow!, Ouch!, Whomp!, Ick!,* and *Gadzooks!*

When we ask for specific words, like a NUMBER, a COLOR, an ANIMAL, or a PART OF THE BODY, we mean a word that is one of those things, like *seven, blue, horse,* or *head.*

When we ask for a PLURAL, it means more than one. For example, *cat* pluralized is *cats.*

MAD LIBS® is fun to play with friends, but you can also play it by yourself! To begin with, DO NOT look at the story on the page below. Fill in the blanks on this page with the words called for. Then, using the words you have selected, fill in the blank spaces in the story.

Now you've created your own hilarious MAD LIBS® game!

DREAMING OF A BACKSTAGE PASS

ADJECTIVE _____

EXCLAMATION _____

LETTER OF THE ALPHABET _____

A PLACE _____

CELEBRITY _____

OCCUPATION _____

VERB ENDING IN "ING" _____

ADJECTIVE _____

ANIMAL _____

CELEBRITY _____

TYPE OF BUILDING _____

VERB _____

VERB ENDING IN "ING" _____

PLURAL NOUN _____

NOUN _____

TYPE OF CONTAINER _____

VERB _____

VERB _____

MAD LIBS®
DREAMING OF
A BACKSTAGE PASS

From one _____ -fan to another . . . _____ !
　　　　　　ADJECTIVE　　　　　　　　　　　　　　　EXCLAMATION

O-M- _____ ! I had an amazing dream last night. I
　　　LETTER OF THE ALPHABET

dreamed I won a back- _____ pass to meet _____ .
　　　　　　　　　　　　　A PLACE　　　　　　　　　　CELEBRITY

She is my favorite _____ ever! In my dream I was literally
　　　　　　　　　　OCCUPATION

_____ up and down like a/an _____
VERB ENDING IN "ING"　　　　　　　　　　　　　　ADJECTIVE

_____ . _____ was so nice in person. We met up
　ANIMAL　　　　　　CELEBRITY

in the _____ 's basement. _____ it or not,
　　　TYPE OF BUILDING　　　　　　　　　VERB

that's where the _____ rooms for all the performers
　　　　　　　　VERB ENDING IN "ING"

are. While I was in the dressing room, we exchanged friendship

_____ and I even got a signed _____
　PLURAL NOUN　　　　　　　　　　　　　　　　　NOUN

that I put in my see-through _____ . Then,
　　　　　　　　　　　　　　TYPE OF CONTAINER

we took a photo together. We both made silly faces in the picture

that made us _____ for hours. What a great dream!
　　　　　　　VERB

If I had amazing dreams like this every night, I'd never want to

_____ up!
　VERB

MAD LIBS® is fun to play with friends, but you can also play it by yourself! To begin with, DO NOT look at the story on the page below. Fill in the blanks on this page with the words called for. Then, using the words you have selected, fill in the blank spaces in the story.

Now you've created your own hilarious MAD LIBS® game!

QUIZ: WHAT ERA ARE YOU IN?

ADJECTIVE _____

COLOR _____

A PLACE _____

ARTICLE OF CLOTHING _____

VERB ENDING IN "ING" _____

ADJECTIVE _____

SOMETHING ALIVE _____

ADJECTIVE _____

PART OF THE BODY _____

PLURAL NOUN _____

ADJECTIVE _____

CITY _____

VEHICLE _____

COLOR _____

ARTICLE OF CLOTHING _____

TYPE OF LIQUID _____

NUMBER _____

CITY _____

MAD LIBS
QUIZ: WHAT ERA ARE YOU IN?

1. What's your favorite thing to wear? (a) a/an _____ coat
   ADJECTIVE
   for walking through a pumpkin patch, (b) an old _____
   COLOR
   sweater you forgot at (the) _____ , (c) a sparkly
   A PLACE
   _____ for _____ in
   ARTICLE OF CLOTHING   VERB ENDING IN "ING"

2. What's your dream job? (a) a/an _____ writer, (b) a florist
   ADJECTIVE
   famous for their _____ arrangements, (c) a dancer
   SOMETHING ALIVE
   famous for a move called the _____ _____
   ADJECTIVE   PART OF THE BODY

3. What's your dream home? (a) a house on a farm where you can
   paint _____ , (b) a/an _____ cottage in
   PLURAL NOUN   ADJECTIVE
   the woods, (c) a penthouse in _____
   CITY

Answer Key: Mostly *a*'s: You're in your "autumn road trip in a/an

_____ and _____ scarf era." Mostly
VEHICLE   COLOR

b's: You're in your "cozy _____ and drinking hot
ARTICLE OF CLOTHING

_____ era." Mostly *c*'s: You're in your "hanging with
TYPE OF LIQUID

_____ friends in _____ era."
NUMBER   CITY

MAD LIBS® is fun to play with friends, but you can also play it by yourself! To begin with, DO NOT look at the story on the page below. Fill in the blanks on this page with the words called for. Then, using the words you have selected, fill in the blank spaces in the story.

Now you've created your own hilarious MAD LIBS® game!

INVITE TO A
POP STAR-THEMED PARTY

CELEBRITY _____

ADJECTIVE _____

SILLY WORD _____

ADJECTIVE _____

VERB _____

NOUN _____

TYPE OF FOOD (PLURAL) _____

TYPE OF CONTAINER _____

TYPE OF EVENT _____

TYPE OF BUILDING _____

SILLY WORD _____

SAME CELEBRITY _____

PART OF THE BODY _____

NOUN _____

ADJECTIVE _____

PLURAL NOUN _____

ADJECTIVE _____

MAD LIBS
INVITE TO A
POP STAR-THEMED PARTY

It's _____'s birthday, and you're invited to our
       CELEBRITY

_____-star birthday bash-a-_____!
   ADJECTIVE   SILLY WORD

We'll have lots of _____ tunes to dance to, plenty of
              ADJECTIVE

_____-along fun, and even a karaoke _____!
  VERB   NOUN

Plus, we'll eat lots of _____ using our fave singer's
             TYPE OF FOOD (PLURAL)

signature recipes. Feel free to bring something yummy to add to the

_____-luck! The _____ starts at 7:00 p.m.
TYPE OF CONTAINER   TYPE OF EVENT

at our _____, at 1989 _____ Street.
     TYPE OF BUILDING   SILLY WORD

Just look for the giant balloon shaped like _____'s
                         SAME CELEBRITY

_____ on the front _____. Dress is
PART OF THE BODY   NOUN

_____. But costumes inspired by one of our star's iconic
ADJECTIVE

_____ are encouraged! Be there or be _____!
PLURAL NOUN   ADJECTIVE

MAD LIBS® is fun to play with friends, but you can also play it by yourself! To begin with, DO NOT look at the story on the page below. Fill in the blanks on this page with the words called for. Then, using the words you have selected, fill in the blank spaces in the story.

Now you've created your own hilarious MAD LIBS® game!

THINGS YOU SHOULD NEVER TOLERATE

NOUN _____

ADJECTIVE _____

TYPE OF EVENT _____

TYPE OF FOOD (PLURAL) _____

PART OF THE BODY _____

VERB _____

ANIMAL _____

VERB _____

TYPE OF EVENT _____

ADJECTIVE _____

ARTICLE OF CLOTHING _____

ANIMAL (PLURAL) _____

ADJECTIVE _____

A PLACE _____

COLOR _____

VERB _____

PLURAL NOUN _____

MAD LIBS®
THINGS YOU SHOULD NEVER TOLERATE

- People who talk over a/an _____ -ball game
  NOUN

- People who think they're more _____ than everyone else
  ADJECTIVE

- People who ruin your _____
  TYPE OF EVENT

- People who tell you that you smell like _____
  TYPE OF FOOD (PLURAL)

- People who break your _____
  PART OF THE BODY

- People who _____ like a/an _____
  VERB   ANIMAL

- People who don't let you _____ at a/an _____
  VERB   TYPE OF EVENT

- People who steal your _____ _____
  ADJECTIVE   ARTICLE OF CLOTHING

- People who don't like _____
  ANIMAL (PLURAL)

- People who make you feel bad for being _____
  ADJECTIVE

- People who ditch you at (the) _____
  A PLACE

- People who hate the color _____
  COLOR

- People who _____ your _____ on the
  VERB   PLURAL NOUN

playground

MAD LIBS® is fun to play with friends, but you can also play it by yourself! To begin with, DO NOT look at the story on the page below. Fill in the blanks on this page with the words called for. Then, using the words you have selected, fill in the blank spaces in the story.

Now you've created your own hilarious MAD LIBS® game!

FROM THE _____ SONG
NOUN

CELEBRITY _____

NOUN _____

ADJECTIVE _____

COLOR _____

CELEBRITY _____

ADJECTIVE _____

ANIMAL _____

VERB _____

PART OF THE BODY _____

ADJECTIVE _____

PLURAL NOUN _____

ARTICLE OF CLOTHING _____

TYPE OF FOOD _____

TYPE OF LIQUID _____

SILLY WORD _____

A PLACE _____

VERB _____

VERB ENDING IN "ING" _____

MAD LIBS®

FROM THE _____ SONG
####### NOUN

I wrote a song to try and be like _____ . Check it out:
######## CELEBRITY

I'm like a/an _____ in a/an _____ part
############# NOUN ################ ADJECTIVE

of New York City.

Everything is _____ when the sun is pretty.
################ COLOR

You're too handsome like _____ ,
############################ CELEBRITY

but you're _____ like a/an _____ .
########### ADJECTIVE ################ ANIMAL

I just want to _____ when you come around.
################ VERB

My _____ makes a desperate sound.
PART OF THE BODY

You're _____ like an army of _____ .
####### ADJECTIVE ########################### PLURAL NOUN

I'm soft and delicate like a/an _____ .
############################### ARTICLE OF CLOTHING

We go together like _____ and _____ .
#################### TYPE OF FOOD ############ TYPE OF LIQUID

We make everyone around us whisper _____ .
################################## SILLY WORD

One day, we'll escape to (the) _____ where
############################### A PLACE

no one can _____ us,
############ VERB

but for now, let's go _____ and make a fuss.
##################### VERB ENDING IN "ING"

MAD LIBS® is fun to play with friends, but you can also play it by yourself! To begin with, DO NOT look at the story on the page below. Fill in the blanks on this page with the words called for. Then, using the words you have selected, fill in the blank spaces in the story.

Now you've created your own hilarious MAD LIBS® game!

DOS AND DON'TS OF GOING TO A CONCERT

TYPE OF EVENT _____

TYPE OF LIQUID _____

NOUN _____

A PLACE _____

ARTICLE OF CLOTHING (PLURAL) _____

PART OF THE BODY (PLURAL) _____

PLURAL NOUN _____

NOUN _____

ADJECTIVE _____

VEHICLE _____

ADJECTIVE _____

VERB _____

VERB _____

ANIMAL _____

CELEBRITY _____

COLOR _____

MAD LIBS®
DOS AND DON'TS OF
GOING TO A CONCERT

Here are some things you need to know if you're going to a big

_____ .
TYPE OF EVENT

1. **Don't** drink too much _____ . You don't want to
    TYPE OF LIQUID

    miss your favorite _____ because you're in (the)
    NOUN

    _____ .
    A PLACE

2. **Don't** wear uncomfortable _____ .
    ARTICLE OF CLOTHING (PLURAL)

3. **Do** protect your _____ with ear-_____ ,
    PART OF THE BODY (PLURAL)   PLURAL NOUN

    because it gets really loud!

4. **Do** bring a cell _____ to capture all the _____
    NOUN   ADJECTIVE

    memories.

5. **Don't** take a/an _____ to the show. The stadium is so
    VEHICLE

    _____ , you'll never find a place to _____ it.
    ADJECTIVE   VERB

6. **Do** _____ your tickets or they won't let you in.
    VERB

7. **Don't** bring your _____ . _____ is allergic,
    ANIMAL   CELEBRITY

    and they're sitting next to you!

8. **Do** represent your favorite album by wearing _____ .
    COLOR

MAD LIBS® is fun to play with friends, but you can also play it by yourself! To begin with, DO NOT look at the story on the page below. Fill in the blanks on this page with the words called for. Then, using the words you have selected, fill in the blank spaces in the story.

Now you've created your own hilarious MAD LIBS® game!

GETTING THE TICKETS

VERB _____

NUMBER _____

EXCLAMATION _____

ADJECTIVE _____

CELEBRITY _____

TYPE OF EVENT _____

OCCUPATION _____

NUMBER _____

NUMBER _____

CITY _____

COLOR _____

ARTICLE OF CLOTHING _____

EXCLAMATION _____

A PLACE _____

VERB _____

FIRST NAME _____

ADJECTIVE _____

PART OF THE BODY _____

MAD LIBS®

GETTING THE TICKETS

Friend #1: Stay calm and don't _____! We are number
_____ in the queue for tickets.
    VERB
NUMBER

Friend #2: _____! This _____ computer better
    EXCLAMATION   *ADJECTIVE*
not crash like it did for _____'s _____.
        CELEBRITY   *TYPE OF EVENT*

Friend #1: That was horrible! We had to get tickets from a/an
_____, and they were _____ feet from the stage.
OCCUPATION   *NUMBER*

Friend #2: We need _____ tickets for the show in _____.
       NUMBER   *CITY*
I already have my _____ outfit planned. Do you want to see
       COLOR
my new _____?
    ARTICLE OF CLOTHING

Friend #1: No time for exclusive concert T-shirts! _____!
                             EXCLAMATION
The computer froze. We might have to send you to (the) _____
                                          A PLACE
for our tickets.

Friend #2: Oh no! I'm going to _____. Heavens to
                                   VERB
_____, let us in!!
FIRST NAME

Friend #1: I'm back online! And we got _____ seats.
                                   ADJECTIVE

Friend #2: I'm so excited, I can't feel my _____.
                                    PART OF THE BODY

called for. Then, using the words you have
selected, fill in the blank spaces in the story.

Now you've created your own hilarious MAD LIBS® game!

WHY CATS RULE

ANIMAL (PLURAL) _____

CELEBRITY _____

SILLY WORD _____

TYPE OF FOOD _____

ARTICLE OF CLOTHING _____

ADJECTIVE _____

NOUN _____

PLURAL NOUN _____

TYPE OF LIQUID _____

PART OF THE BODY _____

TYPE OF CONTAINER _____

VERB _____

ADJECTIVE _____

PLURAL NOUN _____

VERB _____

TYPE OF BUILDING _____

NUMBER _____

MAD LIBS®

WHY CATS RULE

Cats are better than _____! That's why _____
ANIMAL (PLURAL)   CELEBRITY

loves cats, and so should you! Here's why: Cats can be named funny

things like _____ or _____. Do you get cold?
SILLY WORD   TYPE OF FOOD

If your cat sleeps on your _____, it will be warm and
ARTICLE OF CLOTHING

_____. Hate your _____? Your cat can destroy
ADJECTIVE   NOUN

old furniture easily with its sharp _____ and then you
PLURAL NOUN

can get a new one guilt-free. Cats are scared of _____,
TYPE OF LIQUID

but they love when you scratch their _____. Cats
PART OF THE BODY

like to fit into small spaces, so you might catch them sleeping in a/an

_____. Cats don't need to go outside, so you'll never have
TYPE OF CONTAINER

to take them out to _____ when it's _____
VERB   ADJECTIVE

out. What a treat! Cats love to play with _____ and
PLURAL NOUN

_____ all around your _____. And cats have
VERB   TYPE OF BUILDING

_____ lives, so they're always lucky. Cats are purr-fect!
NUMBER

MAD LIBS® is fun to play with friends, but you can also play it by yourself! To begin with, DO NOT look at the story on the page below. Fill in the blanks on this page with the words called for. Then, using the words you have selected, fill in the blank spaces in the story.

Now you've created your own hilarious MAD LIBS® game!

DELICIOUS COOKIE RECIPE

TYPE OF FOOD _____

NUMBER _____

A PLACE _____

TYPE OF FOOD _____

VERB _____

NOUN _____

VERB _____

NOUN _____

TYPE OF CONTAINER _____

TYPE OF LIQUID _____

ADJECTIVE _____

VERB _____

NOUN _____

ADVERB _____

NOUN _____

VERB _____

ADJECTIVE _____

NUMBER _____

MAD LIBS

DELICIOUS COOKIE RECIPE

INGREDIENTS: 3 cups of _____, _____ pounds
　　　　　　　　　　　　　TYPE OF FOOD　　　　　NUMBER

of sugar, 6 _____-fresh eggs, _____ tea, 3 cups
　　　　　　　　A PLACE　　　　　　　　TYPE OF FOOD

of milk, ground cinnamon.

DIRECTIONS: _____ the oven to 350 degrees. Don't
　　　　　　　　　　VERB

forget to line the cookie _____ with parchment paper so
　　　　　　　　　　　　　　NOUN

the cookies don't _____! While the _____
　　　　　　　　　VERB　　　　　　　　　　　　　NOUN

heats up, use a large _____ to mix the flour and
　　　　　　　　　　TYPE OF CONTAINER

sugar for about 1 minute until combined. Add in the tea, the

_____, and 2 teaspoons of _____ cinnamon
TYPE OF LIQUID　　　　　　　　　　　ADJECTIVE

and _____ with a high-powered _____. Add in
　　　　VERB　　　　　　　　　　　　　　　NOUN

the eggs and then stir _____ with a/an _____.
　　　　　　　　　　　ADVERB　　　　　　　　　NOUN

But don't _____ too much! The dough should be
　　　　　　　VERB

_____. Finally, roll into small dough balls and bake for
ADJECTIVE

_____ minutes. Enjoy!
NUMBER

MAD LIBS® is fun to play with friends, but you can also play it by yourself! To begin with, DO NOT look at the story on the page below. Fill in the blanks on this page with the words called for. Then, using the words you have selected, fill in the blank spaces in the story.

Now you've created your own hilarious MAD LIBS® game!

FALL TOO WELL

EXCLAMATION _____

ADJECTIVE _____

CITY _____

PLURAL NOUN _____

ARTICLE OF CLOTHING _____

A PLACE _____

TYPE OF LIQUID _____

TYPE OF FOOD _____

VEHICLE _____

ADJECTIVE _____

ANIMAL _____

VERB ENDING IN "ING" _____

ADJECTIVE _____

PERSON YOU KNOW _____

VERB _____

COLOR _____

VERB _____

NOUN _____

MAD LIBS

FALL TOO WELL

_____! It's a/an _____ fall day in
        EXCLAMATION   ADJECTIVE

_____ and you have a long list of _____
        CITY   PLURAL NOUN

to celebrate. Throw on your cozy _____ and head to
                                    ARTICLE OF CLOTHING

your local _____. You'll sip on hot _____,
              A PLACE   TYPE OF LIQUID

eat freshly baked _____, and go for a hayride on a/an
                      TYPE OF FOOD

_____. Maybe you'll even see a/an _____
        VEHICLE   ADJECTIVE

_____! Next you can go _____ through
        ANIMAL   VERB ENDING IN "ING"

a/an _____ corn maze with _____ and even
          ADJECTIVE   PERSON YOU KNOW

_____ in the colorful piles of leaves. Don't forget to pick
        VERB

your own _____ pumpkin to take home! And then, maybe
              COLOR

you'll be inspired to _____ a new song about it all, using
                          VERB

your favorite _____!
                  NOUN

MAD LIBS® is fun to play with friends, but you can also play it by yourself! To begin with, DO NOT look at the story on the page below. Fill in the blanks on this page with the words called for. Then, using the words you have selected, fill in the blank spaces in the story.

Now you've created your own hilarious MAD LIBS® game!

A LETTER

CELEBRITY _____

ADJECTIVE _____

OCCUPATION (PLURAL) _____

VERB _____

FIRST NAME _____

PART OF THE BODY _____

VERB (PAST TENSE) _____

COLOR _____

NOUN _____

ADJECTIVE _____

TYPE OF EVENT _____

NOUN _____

PART OF THE BODY _____

VERB ENDING IN "ING" _____

NUMBER _____

PLURAL NOUN _____

TYPE OF FOOD _____

ADJECTIVE _____

MAD LIBS®

A LETTER

Dear _____,
     CELEBRITY

It's been a/an _____ summer without you. I've been hit
        ADJECTIVE

by the _____ arrow. I hope I never _____
  OCCUPATION (PLURAL)   VERB

you. If I did, I'd never walk to _____ Street again. My
                           FIRST NAME

_____ has been _____. I thought love was
 PART OF THE BODY   VERB (PAST TENSE)

_____, but now I know it's not. What have you been up
    COLOR

to this summer? I met a/an _____. It's _____
                NOUN   ADJECTIVE

to have a buddy. But I miss you! I kept the _____ lights
                          TYPE OF EVENT

up that we hung together. I've made you a paper _____ to
                             NOUN

put on your _____. Can't wait to give it to you. Waiting
     PART OF THE BODY

to see you again feels like _____ as fast as I can. It's
           VERB ENDING IN "ING"

awful! It also feels like having _____ _____. You're
          NUMBER   PLURAL NOUN

sweeter than _____.
    TYPE OF FOOD

Love,

T. _____
   ADJECTIVE

MAD LIBS® is fun to play with friends, but you can also play it by yourself! To begin with, DO NOT look at the story on the page below. Fill in the blanks on this page with the words called for. Then, using the words you have selected, fill in the blank spaces in the story.

Now you've created your own hilarious MAD LIBS® game!

THE NEXT ERA

NOUN _____

NOUN _____

COLOR _____

NUMBER _____

CELEBRITY _____

CITY _____

VERB _____

VERB _____

VERB ENDING IN "ING" _____

EXCLAMATION _____

PART OF THE BODY _____

ADJECTIVE _____

TYPE OF LIQUID _____

A PLACE _____

OCCUPATION _____

COUNTRY _____

MAD LIBS®

THE NEXT ERA

Did you see the latest post on Insta-_____? A new album
                                       NOUN

is coming! The album's title is _____ and it has a/an
                                        NOUN

_____ cover. The album has _____ songs on
        COLOR   NUMBER

it! Apparently, the first single is a song about the singer's best friend,

_____, and their summer living in _____ together. I
     CELEBRITY   CITY

heard this album is supposed to make us all want to _____,
                                                          VERB

but also _____. I hope it keeps us _____
              VERB   VERB ENDING IN "ING"

for the rest of our lives. There's a brand-new dance anthem called

"_____." It has a dance to go with it where you shake
    EXCLAMATION

your _____ during the chorus. There is also a really
         PART OF THE BODY

_____ song called "_____ Dreams" that was
     ADJECTIVE   TYPE OF LIQUID

recorded in (the) _____. They had someone who is a/an
                      A PLACE

_____ there the whole time to make sure the album was
     OCCUPATION

perfect. They are going to debut the new album at a huge concert in

_____. I bet this means a new tour is coming up!
     COUNTRY

MAD LIBS® is fun to play with friends, but you can also play it by yourself! To begin with, DO NOT look at the story on the page below. Fill in the blanks on this page with the words called for. Then, using the words you have selected, fill in the blank spaces in the story.

Now you've created your own hilarious MAD LIBS® game!

A DAY IN THE LIFE OF A SUPERFAN

CELEBRITY _____

NUMBER _____

NUMBER _____

EXCLAMATION _____

VERB _____

ADJECTIVE _____

ARTICLE OF CLOTHING _____

COLOR _____

ADJECTIVE _____

PART OF THE BODY (PLURAL) _____

VERB ENDING IN "ING" _____

FIRST NAME _____

ADJECTIVE _____

VERB _____

VEHICLE _____

PERSON YOU KNOW _____

VERB _____

ADVERB _____

MAD LIBS®
A DAY IN THE LIFE
OF A SUPERFAN

It's the big day! _____ is coming to my town for show
CELEBRITY

#_____ on their tour, which I've seen _____ times! I don't
NUMBER NUMBER

want to miss any performances! Here's how I get ready. First, I yell

"_____! It's time to _____." Then, I pick out
EXCLAMATION VERB

my _____ _____ in my favorite shade
ADJECTIVE ARTICLE OF CLOTHING

of _____. I always wear my most _____ pair
COLOR ADJECTIVE

of shoes, so my _____ don't hurt from all that
PART OF THE BODY (PLURAL)

_____. I always leave plenty early for the concert so I
VERB ENDING IN "ING"

can get all the best _____ merch, because the lines will be
FIRST NAME

_____ and everything is going to _____ out. In
ADJECTIVE VERB

fact, I should probably leave now! Let's get in your _____
VEHICLE

with _____ and _____ fast. I can't wait to
PERSON YOU KNOW VERB

sing super- _____ the entire concert!
ADVERB

MAD LIBS® is fun to play with friends, but you can also play it by yourself! To begin with, DO NOT look at the story on the page below. Fill in the blanks on this page with the words called for. Then, using the words you have selected, fill in the blank spaces in the story.

Now you've created your own hilarious MAD LIBS® game!

BEJEWELED AFFIRMATIONS

EXCLAMATION _____

ADJECTIVE _____

CELEBRITY _____

VEHICLE _____

CITY _____

ADJECTIVE _____

NUMBER _____

PERSON YOU KNOW _____

TYPE OF FOOD _____

SILLY WORD _____

TYPE OF BUILDING _____

CITY _____

TYPE OF LIQUID _____

NOUN _____

COLOR _____

VERB _____

EXCLAMATION _____

MAD LIBS®

BEJEWELED AFFIRMATIONS

Say the following to yourself in the mirror:

- _____! I am so _____. Everyone wants to be
  EXCLAMATION   ADJECTIVE

  my friend, even _____.
                    CELEBRITY

- I am going to plaster my face on the side of a/an _____
                                                        VEHICLE

  so everyone in _____ can admire me.
                    CITY

- I am a/an _____ friend. That's why I have _____
              ADJECTIVE   NUMBER

  friends! My best friend, _____, can tell you how
                            PERSON YOU KNOW

  awesome I am.

- I naturally smell like _____, and they're making
                          TYPE OF FOOD

  a perfume that smells like me called _____. How
                                        SILLY WORD

  exciting!

- One day, I am going to live in a/an _____
                                        TYPE OF BUILDING

  in _____ with a pool of _____.
      CITY   TYPE OF LIQUID

- I shine as bright as a/an _____! I am made of
                              NOUN

  _____ glitter and sunshine! Every day I _____
   COLOR   VERB

  around my house and scream " _____!"
                                EXCLAMATION

MAD LIBS® is fun to play with friends, but you can also play it by yourself! To begin with, DO NOT look at the story on the page below. Fill in the blanks on this page with the words called for. Then, using the words you have selected, fill in the blank spaces in the story.

Now you've created your own hilarious MAD LIBS® game!

FASHION STORY

ADJECTIVE _____

NOUN _____

COLOR _____

NUMBER _____

COUNTRY _____

ADJECTIVE _____

TYPE OF EVENT _____

CELEBRITY _____

ADVERB _____

CITY _____

ANIMAL _____

ARTICLE OF CLOTHING _____

TYPE OF FOOD _____

PART OF THE BODY _____

ADJECTIVE _____

A PLACE _____

VERB ENDING IN "ING" _____

PERSON YOU KNOW _____

MAD LIBS®

FASHION STORY

If you want to dress like a star, here are some _____ pieces
ADJECTIVE

to make you shine like the _____! First, you'll need a pair
NOUN

of _____ boots with the lucky number _____ bedazzled
COLOR   NUMBER

on them in rhinestones, from a fancy store in _____.
COUNTRY

Then, you'll need a/an _____ ball gown. It should be perfect
ADJECTIVE

for a/an _____. You'll also need a scarf—but don't
TYPE OF EVENT

let _____ steal it! And don't forget sunglasses to wear
CELEBRITY

_____ as you explore _____. Of course, you'll need
ADVERB   CITY

an outfit inspired by the mischievous animal that inspired an entire

album . . . the _____. You'll need a pink _____
ANIMAL   ARTICLE OF CLOTHING

covered in hearts to make you look sweeter than _____. To
TYPE OF FOOD

keep your _____ warm, you'll need a/an _____
PART OF THE BODY   ADJECTIVE

sweater, perfect for wearing out in a forest or even wearing to (the)

_____. To complete your wardrobe, you'll need a sparkly
A PLACE

coat perfect for _____ at a party late at night with
VERB ENDING IN "ING"

_____.
PERSON YOU KNOW

MAD LIBS® is fun to play with friends, but you can also play it by yourself! To begin with, DO NOT look at the story on the page below. Fill in the blanks on this page with the words called for. Then, using the words you have selected, fill in the blank spaces in the story.

Now you've created your own hilarious MAD LIBS® game!

NIGHT OUT!

CELEBRITY _____

CITY _____

ARTICLE OF CLOTHING _____

VEHICLE _____

TYPE OF EVENT _____

EXCLAMATION _____

CELEBRITY _____

PERSON YOU KNOW _____

PART OF THE BODY _____

TYPE OF LIQUID _____

A PLACE _____

VERB _____

ADJECTIVE _____

NUMBER _____

NOUN _____

VERB _____

NOUN _____

ADJECTIVE _____

MAD LIBS

NIGHT OUT!

You and your best friend, _____, are out on the town in
                              CELEBRITY

_____. You're wearing your favorite _____
        CITY   ARTICLE OF CLOTHING

and getting in your _____ to go to the next _____.
                          VEHICLE   TYPE OF EVENT

_____! _____ is here, too, with _____.
   EXCLAMATION   CELEBRITY   PERSON YOU KNOW

You shake their _____ and introduce yourself. They offer
                  PART OF THE BODY

you a glass of _____. You ask if they've been to (the)
                  TYPE OF LIQUID

_____ and decide it's time to hit the dance floor and
     A PLACE

_____. It's _____ because there's too many people
     VERB   ADJECTIVE

in the room. In fact, there are _____ people in the room! That's
                                     NUMBER

way too many! There's a stunning person in the corner who looks

like a/an _____. They ask you to _____, so you get
              NOUN   VERB

shaking. At the end of the night, you hand them your _____
                                                            NOUN

so they can write their name and number. What a fun night out, full

of old friends and _____ friends!
                        ADJECTIVE

MAD LIBS® is fun to play with friends, but you can also play it by yourself! To begin with, DO NOT look at the story on the page below. Fill in the blanks on this page with the words called for. Then, using the words you have selected, fill in the blank spaces in the story.

Now you've created your own hilarious MAD LIBS® game!

LUCKY NUMBER

NUMBER _____

CELEBRITY _____

NOUN _____

NOUN _____

VERB _____

PART OF THE BODY _____

LAST NAME _____

CITY _____

VERB ENDING IN "ING" _____

ADJECTIVE _____

COLOR _____

SOMETHING ALIVE _____

PLURAL NOUN _____

TYPE OF EVENT _____

NOUN _____

SAME NUMBER _____

SAME NUMBER _____

ADJECTIVE _____

MAD LIBS®

LUCKY NUMBER

There are so many reasons why _____ is _____ 's favorite
                                    NUMBER   CELEBRITY

number! Maybe it's just a/an _____ , maybe it's fate, but that
                                   NOUN

number keeps popping up in the star's _____—and not just
                                              NOUN

because they _____ it onto their _____ before
                   VERB   PART OF THE BODY

every concert. It was also the age when the _____ family
                                                   LAST NAME

moved to _____ , Tennessee, and started _____
              CITY   VERB ENDING IN "ING"

_____ music. And it was the number of weeks it took
     ADJECTIVE

for the singer's first album to go _____. It's even the
                                          COLOR

_____ 's birthday! The star has even said in numerous
   SOMETHING ALIVE

televised _____ that every time they go to an award-
               PLURAL NOUN

winning _____ , they're sitting in a seat or _____
            TYPE OF EVENT   NOUN

that is number _____ . Sounds like the number _____
                   SAME NUMBER   SAME NUMBER

isn't so _____ after all!
              ADJECTIVE

MAD LIBS® is fun to play with friends, but you can also play it by yourself! To begin with, DO NOT look at the story on the page below. Fill in the blanks on this page with the words called for. Then, using the words you have selected, fill in the blank spaces in the story.

Now you've created your own hilarious MAD LIBS® game!

FAVORITE SONG

NOUN _____

VERB _____

ADJECTIVE _____

CITY _____

VERB (PAST TENSE) _____

NOUN _____

PART OF THE BODY _____

NUMBER _____

VERB ENDING IN "ING" _____

VERB _____

COLOR _____

TYPE OF BUILDING _____

COLOR _____

VERB _____

NUMBER _____

ADJECTIVE _____

VERB _____

PLURAL NOUN _____

MAD LIBS

FAVORITE SONG

Whether you like _____ music, pop, hip-_____, or
NOUN   VERB

_____ metal, everyone from Los Angeles to _____
ADJECTIVE   CITY

has a favorite song! I can remember the first time I heard the song

"I _____ You Were _____." The memory
VERB (PAST TENSE)   NOUN

is so clear in my _____, it's like I just heard the song
PART OF THE BODY

_____ days ago. I was _____ in line to buy some
NUMBER   VERB ENDING IN "ING"

albums by the bands Cold-_____ and _____ 5
VERB   COLOR

when the song came on the radio. I dropped those albums and ran to

the back of the _____ to pick up the _____
TYPE OF BUILDING   COLOR

album instead! I knew I had to _____ that album right
VERB

then and there! And _____ years later, I still listen to that song
NUMBER

whenever I'm feeling _____! And you know what, it always
ADJECTIVE

makes me _____ better! Even on days when I just want to
VERB

throw my _____ up and scream!
PLURAL NOUN

MAD LIBS® is fun to play with friends, but you can also play it by yourself! To begin with, DO NOT look at the story on the page below. Fill in the blanks on this page with the words called for. Then, using the words you have selected, fill in the blank spaces in the story.

Now you've created your own hilarious MAD LIBS® game!

BONDING OVER BRACELETS

CITY _____

VERB _____

A PLACE _____

COLOR _____

ANIMAL _____

VERB _____

CITY _____

NOUN _____

NOUN _____

TYPE OF LIQUID _____

ADJECTIVE _____

NOUN _____

NOUN _____

VEHICLE _____

VERB ENDING IN "ING" _____

PART OF THE BODY (PLURAL) _____

MAD LIBS®
BONDING OVER BRACELETS

Make bracelets to trade with other fans based on these hit songs:

- "Welcome to _____"
  CITY

- "_____ It Off"
  VERB

- "Girl at (the) _____"
  A PLACE

- "_____ _____"
  COLOR   ANIMAL

- "_____ Then Fall"
  VERB

- "_____ Boy"
  CITY

- "Message in a/an _____"
  NOUN

- "The Other Side of the _____"
  NOUN

- "_____ Problems"
  TYPE OF LIQUID

- "The _____ One"
  ADJECTIVE

- "Cruel _____"
  NOUN

- "_____ Story"
  NOUN

- "Getaway _____"
  VEHICLE

- "_____ with Our _____ Tied"
  VERB ENDING IN "ING"   PART OF THE BODY (PLURAL)

MAD LIBS® is fun to play with friends, but you can also play it by yourself! To begin with, DO NOT look at the story on the page below. Fill in the blanks on this page with the words called for. Then, using the words you have selected, fill in the blank spaces in the story.

Now you've created your own hilarious MAD LIBS® game!

BREAKING NEWS

EXCLAMATION _____

CELEBRITY _____

VERB (PAST TENSE) _____

TYPE OF EVENT _____

ADVERB _____

SAME CELEBRITY _____

TYPE OF LIQUID _____

ANIMAL _____

VERB (PAST TENSE) _____

ADJECTIVE _____

COLOR _____

ARTICLE OF CLOTHING _____

EXCLAMATION _____

VEHICLE _____

OCCUPATION _____

ADJECTIVE _____

YOUR NAME _____

NOUN _____

MAD LIBS®

BREAKING NEWS

_____! _____ _____ at
EXCLAMATION   CELEBRITY   VERB (PAST TENSE)

an exclusive _____. Things are going _____ for
              TYPE OF EVENT   ADVERB

_____. _____ fell on them after a/an
SAME CELEBRITY   TYPE OF LIQUID

_____ _____ through a/an _____
ANIMAL   VERB (PAST TENSE)   ADJECTIVE

party filled with other famous celebrities. Their _____
                                                   COLOR

_____ was ruined. _____! How embarrassing!
ARTICLE OF CLOTHING   EXCLAMATION

They ran back to their _____ crying. They told reporters they
                       VEHICLE

wanted to quit being a celebrity and become a/an _____ after
                                                 OCCUPATION

this _____ night. Luckily, their new crush, _____ ,
     ADJECTIVE   YOUR NAME

a famous _____-ball player, came to the rescue and turned
         NOUN

their night around. It must be nice to have a friend like that!

MAD LIBS® is fun to play with friends, but you can also play it by yourself! To begin with, DO NOT look at the story on the page below. Fill in the blanks on this page with the words called for. Then, using the words you have selected, fill in the blank spaces in the story.

Now you've created your own hilarious MAD LIBS® game!

THE ERRORS TOUR

ADJECTIVE _____

COUNTRY _____

NOUN _____

NUMBER _____

A SOUND _____

OCCUPATION _____

ANIMAL _____

ADJECTIVE _____

PERSON YOU KNOW _____

CELEBRITY _____

EXCLAMATION _____

ADVERB _____

VERB (PAST TENSE) _____

VERB (PAST TENSE) _____

PART OF THE BODY _____

ADJECTIVE _____

MAD LIBS

THE ERRORS TOUR

Uh-oh! Things are _____ at the concert in _____
  (ADJECTIVE)   (COUNTRY)

tonight. First, the grand _____ broke, and _____ dancers
                              (NOUN)   (NUMBER)

tripped during the opening song. Then, the backdrop made a loud

_____ and came crashing down. The _____
  (A SOUND)   (OCCUPATION)

had to stop singing for a moment because she swallowed a/an

_____ . Security got _____ and tried to kick
  (ANIMAL)   (ADJECTIVE)

_____ out for singing along, causing _____
  (PERSON YOU KNOW)   (CELEBRITY)

to shout "_____ !" It started raining and water fell
           (EXCLAMATION)

_____ . The piano _____ , scaring everyone
  (ADVERB)   (VERB (PAST TENSE))

in the stadium. But the show must go on! And it did . . . until the

star slipped and _____ thanks to all the rain. She hurt
                    (VERB (PAST TENSE))

her _____ and had to sing lying down. She still sounded
      (PART OF THE BODY)

_____ , though!
  (ADJECTIVE)